"Not all wounds are so visible,
walk gently in the lives of others"

This booklet is dedicated to my wonderful family:
husband Peter, our children Hayden, Richard, Courtney,
and our unforgotten baby—Hope

Also, my dearest friends who believed in me/us
and gave their unwavering support

Marina & Peter Young
www.buttonsproject.org
© 2018 Marina & Peter Young

Written and published by: Marina & Peter Young, email: marina@buttonsproject.org
Project management: Wild Side Publishing www.wildsidepublishing.com

Cataloguing in Publication Data:
Title: The Unforgotten Babies: The Inspiration Behind the Buttons Project
ISBN: 978-0-473-42819-8 (pbk.)
Subjects: Memoir, Biography, Abortion, Mental Health, Christian Living, Social & Ethical Issues

International listing 2018 Ingram Spark

What people are saying about
The Unforgotten Babies

"I am so grateful to both Marina and Peter for opening up their lives and experience in order that others might hear about the reality of abortion and its effect on women, men, marriages, families, and ultimately, society. This resource speaks truth, and as we know from the Gospel of John, "the truth will set you free". Please read this book – and then share it! Choose life."

Bob McCoskrie
National Director, Family First NZ
www.familyfirst.org.nz

"Unforgotten Babies is the story behind the Buttons Project. A personal story of two people; Marina and Peter Young. Nothing speaks louder than personal experiences and when it comes to the experience of abortion, we know that it takes courage to share one's story.

In reading the booklet, I appreciated the authors' owning and heartfelt expressions of the reality of what happened and what it has meant. What stands out is how abortion is never an isolated event. It happens in the context of each individual's personal history, and the circumstances at the time of the pregnancy as perceived and experienced by each person, and the partnership. This creates an often complex web of influence which plays out over time for two souls genuinely seeking a good outcome to what is a difficult and problematic situation filled with conflict and emotion.

It is often underestimated how much an abortion experience can impact and alter a person. This booklet describes clearly how an abortion can be significant and the effects lasting and widespread. I was deeply struck by Marina's attitude, as an adult mother herself, to her mum, which was aptly reflected in the quote she shared: "Before you start to judge me, step into my shoes and walk the life I'm living, and if you get as far as I am, just maybe you will see how strong I really am."

Also I was moved deeply by Peter's admission of the change in him afterwards. "I realised I needed healing... to acknowledge my failings, admitting my mistakes and seeking... forgiveness." That philosophy, understanding and respect is now demonstrated in Marina and Peter's work with the Buttons Project, where they are able to use their own abortion experience to reach out and support others on their journey of healing. They offer Christ-like love and acceptance in meeting others who are struggling with the loss and trauma of a recent or past experience. And the buttons being collected signify that each life mattered, which is hugely powerful, as abortion remains such a disenfranchised loss.

Thank you Marina and Peter for your willingness to be open about how abortion touched and changed each of you, and you as a couple. I sincerely hope that in reading your booklet, others with similar experiences will feel that they are not alone, and can find hope as you have done. May you be richly blessed as you bless others with the Buttons Project."

Carolina Gnad
Founder & Co-ordinator of Education and Training
P.A.T.H.S. (Post Abortion Trauma Healing Service)
www.postabortionpaths.org.nz | 0800 728 470

"A 'lived experience', written with humble honesty, allowing the reader new insights. A very valuable resource for New Zealand and beyond."

Cushla Hassan BN.NZRCN.
Co-founder & Clinical Nurse Manager
GP based Hapai Taumaha Hapūtanga
Crisis Pregnancy Support
www.crisispregnancysupport.org.nz

"Marina and Peter's story is powerful. It's powerful because they have been so transparent in their explanation of the journey. As a result, those who read this story will find themselves with a sense of comfort within their pain. And for those who are considering abortion, they will find their eyes opened by grace and an opportunity to consider other options. Thank you, Marina and Peter, for your transparency."

Jo Hood
International CEO, mainly music

"I was so impressed with *'The Unforgotten Babies'*, the honesty and transparency was refreshing. It is so helpful for our clients who are facing an unplanned pregnancy to read about someone else's experience. I especially appreciated the chapter from a man's perspective as so often men don't know how to respond. I highly recommend this booklet to anyone facing an unplanned pregnancy or struggling after an abortion."

Janice Tetley-Jones
Director
Pregnancy Choice Centre Tauranga
www.pregnancychoice.org.nz

Contents

Abandonment

1945

On 12th February, 1945 my Mum entered this world. Nana called her Raina and Mum always said it was because it was raining that day.

Mum's dad, my grandfather, had driven Nana to hospital to give birth and then disappeared: she never heard of him again. What a devastating shock for my Nana, to be left to raise three children on her own, and especially tough with it being right at the end of World War Two.

There was no support for the family; Nana had to wait seven years after his disappearance before my grandfather could be declared dead so that she could receive a widow's benefit. Nana died when I was 13, so I will never fully know how she coped in those early years; I have only heard bits and pieces from my aunts and uncle. I know she used to sing in cabarets occasionally (unfortunately I never inherited her good singing voice). Not surprisingly, she lost all trust in men. She was constantly in debt and would send the children to different shops to run an account to get credit. Life

was very hard for her and her family, made even tougher
by hardness in her heart that led to her constantly
reprimanding and scolding her children.

My Mum acutely felt the sense of being abandoned by
her father. Her older siblings were just pre-schoolers
at the time and were totally puzzled—their mother
bringing home a new baby sister but never seeing or
hearing from their dad again.

My aunts and uncle shared stories and rumours about
what had become of my grandfather but we never knew
the truth until a cousin started doing research into the
family tree. Grandad had initially run off with another
woman, faked his death by drowning and then travelled
to England where he raised another family. He never
talked about his first family in New Zealand until he was
on his deathbed in 1998, by which time Nana and my
uncle were dead and my Mum and aunts were all in
their sixties.

His stepson, whom my grandfather had raised as his
own, contacted us years later. Apparently, Grandad was
a wonderful stepfather, which Mum and her siblings
found so hard to comprehend—maybe he was trying
his best to make up for the past. But it was too late to ask
their father why he had done what he did, and my Nana
took a lot of unsaid things to her grave as well. So we will
never fully know the truth but I am sure there would be
many sides to the story.

It is surreal to be in contact with Grandad's stepson, to have a link to that mysterious part of my family's story. I look forward to meeting him in person one day and learning more about my Grandad because, just as my Mum missed out having a father, I feel I missed out having grandparents.

> Just as my Mum missed out having a father, I feel I missed out having grandparents

Against all odds she gave me life

My Mum left school at 14, lied about her age and started work. At 18, she launched into the big wide world, going to Australia with her best friend, Marrilyn. They hitch-hiked, did some exploring and worked for a time in the steel mill café at Wollongong. A lot of Yugoslavs and Greeks worked in the steel mill and Mum met a young Greek gentleman, 'J', and dated him for a few months. However, she struggled with the Greek culture, especially her role as a woman within it. So she travelled further north, with her friend Marrilyn, to Surfers Paradise for a while. She loved the beach and the lifestyle.

Mum's friend Marrilyn stayed in Australia but Mum decided to return to New Zealand. She contacted 'J' by letter for a last catch up before she left. They met

in Sydney, visited the zoo and spent time together.
Mum said they had some kind of argument before she
left, so they parted not on good terms but, unbeknown
to her at that stage, she had conceived and I was being
formed.

Having an
abortion was
not an option
for my Mum

Mum went back home to live
with Nana. When she realised she
was pregnant she was afraid of
how Nana would react. Having
an abortion was not an option for
my Mum. She hid it for as long
as possible but, due to fainting at
work, her pregnancy became known and Nana, in her
anger, ordered her to move out.

Being single and pregnant in the 1960s was frowned
upon and there was not a lot of support available,
so Mum stayed with her sister until I, Marina Sophia
Johnston, was born on 11th November 1965.

Back then, mothers stayed in hospital for up to a
fortnight after giving birth. Because she was a single
unwed mother, she was put in her own room away from
the other mums in case she led them astray! It must
have been a lonely, scary and emotional time for my
Mum, especially with no support from her own mum.
She was only 20 years old at the time.

She left hospital and we stayed with an older couple
(whom Mum said were lovely) for a few months until

I was 8 months old. Mum never told 'J' about the pregnancy, so my father and his family never knew about me. 'J' had said he would write when they parted; maybe he did but, if he did write, it is thought that Nana destroyed the letters. So, again, there are parts of the story we will never know. The older couple did give Mum an option of flying to Australia to tell 'J' but, because of her pride and independent 'can do' attitude, she embarked instead on motherhood on her own. She travelled to Auckland to start a fresh life.

Mum did visit Nana when I was about two years old. Nana's anger had subsided and she spent time with me, her granddaughter. A lot happened in my Mum's family, so many secrets. There was a special bond between Mum, her sisters and (while he was alive) her brother. She still stays close to her sisters; they are all survivors of hardship and the tough upbringing with their mum, my Nana.

Growing up in a blended family is never dull

It was not until I was raising my own family that I fully appreciated my Mum for all that she did in raising me and my siblings. I still do not comprehend some of the decisions she made but I understand that they were

> It was not until I was raising my own family that I fully appreciated my Mum for all that she did in raising me and my siblings

influenced by her upbringing, her life experiences and what she knew at the time. Many of those decisions must have been made out of sheer survival instinct and always out of a belief that she was doing the best thing for us.

I came across this quote which sums up the attitude I have now to my Mum: *"Before you start to judge me, step into my shoes and walk the life I'm living, and if you get as far as I am, just maybe you will see how strong I really am."*

We moved lots of times while I was young—about 30 times before I was seven—and Mum had another baby, Steven. Due to tough times and no father on the scene, Mum thought she would be giving Steven a better life if she let him be adopted.

This decision was not taken lightly. The adopting couple had already adopted a boy and wanted a brother for him. Mum never got to meet the new parents—she just got a glimpse of them through a crack in the door—because, back then, meeting them was not an option. She passed on to the new adoptive parents all of Steven's baby clothes, hoping that they would be able to tell from them that she loved him. She hoped that later on in life they would pass on to Steven the message that he had been loved by his mother.

Mum went on to have another son and saw this as being given a second chance. Again, there was no father involvement and Mum tried her best to raise us as a single parent. Mum never got over putting her first son up for adoption and lived with the deep grief and loss silently within her.

One important thing I never doubt: Mum did love her children and never once said we were a mistake. That is something I am forever thankful for.

> Mum did love her children and never once said we were a mistake

Being an unwed mother in the 1960s and 70s was not easy, for her or for us children. It was certainly not as acceptable as it is today. It was hard going to school not knowing who my father was. I felt so different from the rest of the kids and sometimes felt quite stigmatised.

Because my other baby brother had disappeared, I was a staunch protector of my younger brother. From a young age I became a rescuer of people and animals.

Mum married when I was seven years old and my brother, TJ, was two. My new stepfather had a son and daughter as well. I think Mum was looking for a father for us, and he was looking for a mother for his children. It is hard to know whether they were truly in love, because they never really expressed affection to each other. So: TJ and I gained a step-brother and step-sister and, when I was 13, my kid sister was born. Her birth 'kind of' knitted the family together. A few years back, a counsellor I was seeing asked me to describe my family tree. The counsellor got so confused that she asked me to work it out at home and bring it next time!

Anyway, through all those years, I felt like the black sheep in the family. Being part Greek, I had black hair and the rest of the family were fairer skinned. Our step-sister and step-brother went to stay with their birth mum in the holidays, but TJ and I did not know our fathers and so did not have that connection. They would come home laden with presents. Mum could not afford to give us similar gifts and it would often cause big fights within the family. I would also envy our youngest sister who was being raised by both her mum and her dad.

Sometimes life takes us to places we never expected to go

There was frequent conflict between Mum and my stepfather, often over us kids. There were times when plates and cups would go flying by, before Mum would take off and disappear for hours. Then she would return and carry on as if nothing had happened. Unfortunately, it taught us to run away from problems and not confront them.

I missed out on having a father who encouraged me, hugged me and guided me. So I grew to be a people-pleaser, forever looking for love, acceptance and approval from whoever would give it to me.

Getting to school was scary—all through Intermediate and High

> I grew to be a people-pleaser, forever looking for love, acceptance and approval from whoever would give it to me

School I had to pass a gang house, both going to school and coming home, and it was very intimidating. But at school, I had Indian, Samoan, Māori, Pākehā and Vietnamese friends. I made sure I covered all my bases! One big Māori guy used to always look out for me and be my protector.

I left school at 16 and got into a serious relationship for two years. Through this boyfriend I got involved in speedway, which had a very seedy side: bikers, gangs and dealers. I still craved love and acceptance and so tried to be 'someone else'. In my journey I made some bad choices which still affect me today. I saw how the effects of alcohol and drugs ripple on to impact family and friends. It was a dark time for me. By the age of 18, I had experienced so much in my life and I began to really question where my life was heading.

My lifestyle had ruined many of those great friendships I had at high school; however, I did have one very faithful friend, Rhondda, who kept in contact with me throughout this time. She took me on a youth camp and for once I felt accepted for whom I was and loved. The change in me was automatic and dramatic. I broke up with my long-term boyfriend and left that scene. It was a new beginning. Strangely, my parents found it very hard to accept change, even though I was becoming a better person.

> For once I felt accepted for whom I was and loved

I got involved in drama, went white-water rafting, tramping and dancing. I loved trying all these new things and enjoying life. I realized how oppressive my relationship had been: he had controlled all the money I earned and I do not recall him ever telling me that I looked lovely or treating me with respect.

Then I met Peter. I was nineteen and he had just come back from travelling overseas. He was a fairly new Christian and we started going out. We were the 'ideal couple', but then we slipped up and I thought I was pregnant, so Peter proposed to me and I said, 'yes'. My pregnancy was confirmed. A range of emotions surged through my mind—I actually laughed at the thought of me being a mum; there was excitement but also fear for our relationship. Would it last? Was it true love, or was Peter just acting out of obligation?

My pregnancy was confirmed

At first, Pete was very happy. He arrived with flowers (that impressed the three girls I was flatting with, but I did not feel I could tell them the reason). We tried to work through ways we could afford things. We brought forward the wedding date, so we could 'cover the evidence'. However, Pete began to be spoken to by certain family members. They stressed the reality of the life changes ahead; they urged him to get a quick fix.

I had always been against abortion, even without knowing fully about the procedure and the aftermath of abortion. But we were told that having an unplanned baby would forever be a hindrance. We would always struggle financially. I felt cornered. I was too scared to discuss this with my church-going friends and family. Then I had growing fears that if I had this baby, Pete would leave me and another child would be raised without a father. My personal experience of fatherlessness, and my mother's experience, made this a real fear: to not know your father, to not feel quite complete and to not have a full family heritage to look back on. What a pickle!!

> **I really wanted to do what was best for all those involved**

So I went to see a doctor. I was about 9 weeks along at the time and, as I thought, it was only a foetus—a blob of tissue, easy to discard. Back then I didn't know about Pregnancy Counselling services or what other options I had. The doctor did not offer an alternative like keeping the baby or adopting it out. I can genuinely say I was not just thinking of myself; I really wanted to do what was best for all those involved. So, full of anxieties, I went to the abortion clinic in Epsom. Pete accompanied me.

October 1986—forever imprinted on my mind

I was now 10-12 weeks pregnant and had to go to the Epsom Day Clinic over three days. I lied to my work and said I had a really bad stomach bug.

Day 1: Pete picked me up and came with me. The waiting lounge was full of women of different ages and walks of life. Some were with their boyfriends; some were alone or with their Mum or a friend. No one talked to those around them, because we were all there for the same reason and, deep down, it still just did not seem right.

With four other girls, I was led to a room where a woman explained the termination procedure of the 'foetus'. Funnily enough, the instructor was about 7-8 months pregnant. I thought it must be alright, surely, or why would she be there? They showed how the Doctor would use a suction tube and suck the foetus out. It is as easy as that and it only takes about ten minutes.

Day 2: I had an ultrasound, but I was not shown the picture and I did not know you could hear a heartbeat. I think now that if I had heard the heartbeat, I think I would have known that it was not just an 'unformed blob', but a baby.

> If I had heard the heartbeat, I think I would have known that it was not just an 'unformed blob', but a baby

I then went to another room and saw a counsellor. The father of the baby was never discussed, never brought into consideration; how I was feeling was more important. The counsellor listened to my fears of repeating the past, and that Pete might side with his

parents' views and not want the child. The counsellor
agreed with me: I was doing the right thing and that she
would hold my hand. That was that!

Day 3: Pete drove me once again to the clinic and
waited in the waiting room. I changed into a hospital
gown and entered another waiting room with about 10
hospital beds and young women. And then I was called.
I do not remember being called by name, but rather I felt
like a cow being pushed along in the meat works, like a
number and becoming part of a statistic.
I was told to lie down and my legs were put in stirrups.
No nice words, just matter of fact instructions. It felt
cold. I was given an injection to numb down below and
then the suction started. I was not numbed properly
and felt the pulling and the tearing. It seemed to go on
forever, but it was only about ten minutes—ten minutes
which changed my life forever.

Some truth: I found out later that they do not just suck
out 'a blob'. The vacuum is 29 times more powerful than
a normal vacuum cleaner.[1] The baby was torn limb from
limb. The head is too big to suck out,
so they use a tool like a nutcracker to
crush it, then suck it out with
the placenta.

As the baby was terminated, a part of me died too

Afterwards, walking with difficulty,
I was guided to my bed to rest for
a little while. I passed other girls

---

[1] www.life.org.nz/abortion/aboutabortion/methods1/Default.htm

sobbing theirs hearts out, another was hysterical at the realisation of what had just happened. For me, I went cold and numb. As the baby was terminated, a part of me died too. I used to be a happy go lucky person, but now... who was I? I have destroyed a part of me. What have I done?

Pete drove me home. It was over, now we could get on with our lives. Yeah, right!

Before the termination, while I was arranging the wedding with my Mum, in my despair I told my Mum I was pregnant. She was naturally shocked but, with my hormones and emotions all over the place I really could not tell how Mum had responded to the news. So, I didn't tell Mum about the abortion. I had to say something, so I said that I had a miscarriage. Another lie.

My mum turned up at the flat with flowers and a new nightie for me. I felt even more ashamed. She was grieving for the lost child. With a shock I realised that this baby would have been her first grandchild. If only I had confided more with her. I felt weak as a person, much weaker than her: she had me out of wedlock and, even without support, had shown a willingness to work through the consequences and raise me.

> With a shock I realised this baby would have been her first grandchild

About the time I had the abortion, a friend arrived back from overseas. She, too, was pregnant. However, she decided to keep her baby. Her baby would be born in April which would have been the due date of my baby. Another blow to undermine my confidence that I had made the right decision. I grieved in silence.

In the weeks and months that followed, my emotions were extreme: laughing one minute and then crying. I got a bad infection in my ovaries and was bedridden for days.

Pete and I married on 7th December 1986. Our marriage has been a rocky one. For me, I have had feelings of both love and hate for him. When I was depressed, he would tell me to, 'Get over it! What is done is done!' I know now that many relationships fall apart after an abortion. After an abortion, the rate of marital breakup and relationship dissolution is anywhere from 40 to 75 per cent. It is often attributed to the breakdown of intimacy and trust.[2]

When we felt ready to have another baby, I thought this would help me get over it. However, when I saw the ultrasound of Hayden, with his heart beating and sucking his thumb at 18 weeks, I realised the reality of what we had done. No baby was ever going

No baby was ever going to replace the other one, as they are all unique and have their own identity

[2] *Women's Health after Abortion: The Medical and Psychological Evidence,* by Elizabeth Ring-Cassidy and Ian Gentles

to replace the other one, as they are all unique and have their own identity. Instead of the pregnancy being one of joy, it was tinged with sadness for the baby lost.

It was at this time I sought counselling and endeavoured to move forward. I wanted to love my children and be a good mum. During this time, unbeknown to me, Pete was also going through his own turmoil and regretted his part in it all. That is his story to tell, but he too grieved and found it very hard to talk about, especially as a male.

Pete was also going through his own turmoil and regretted his part in it

Peter and I have now been married more than 30 years. You might say we must have it all together by now and that it all worked out alright in the end. You might think that, given time, maybe it would work out for you, too. I would hope so, but I would never want anyone to go through an abortion: the loss you feel, the empty void, as well as the effects on your relationship with your partner and even the relationships around you.

Having a child a couple of years earlier, would it have made all that much difference? Maybe we

Having a child a couple of years earlier, would it have made all that much difference?

would not have travelled early in our married life, but we could still have travelled later. I am sure we would have had a lot more joy in our lives, instead of the sadness, anger and guilt we have endured. And my health would not have been impacted: I would not have got my infection and the ulcer that followed.

Life would not have been easy with baby, but the road would of been a lot less rocky. It took Pete and I many years to fully move forward. I still grieve the loss of the baby, which we later named Hope; Hope for the future, to be the best we can in all we do and to help others not make the same choice we did.

> It has created a scar in our memories that will forever be present in our minds

It may have been a quick fix, a band aid, but it has created a scar in our memories that will forever be present in our minds. I often look at our three children, who all look very much alike, and wonder what Hope would have looked like. What would she be doing now? What difference would Hope be making in this world?'

A new chapter in my life begins

When my children were young, I was in a desperate state and turned to the wisdom of Scripture. It was the start of a new journey for me. I experienced healing for my past, strength to face the future with hope. I gained a new perspective on life which I wanted to share with those around me. A passion started to build up inside me: to help others not make the same mistakes I did, and to give them a purpose and hope.

The power of passion

"Passion is powerful. Nothing was ever achieved without it and nothing can take its place. No matter what you face in life, if your passion is great enough you will find the strength to succeed. Without passion, life has no meaning, so put your heart, mind and soul into even your smallest acts—this is the essence of passion. This is the secret to life. All your dreams can come true if you will passionately pursue them." [3]

[3] Pastor Barnett, Dreamcenter Los Angeles

I believe it all comes down to timing and preparation. Thirty years ago I would never have thought I would have the confidence and strength to do what I am involved in today.

After doing some Community Work papers at Unitech, I wanted to put my study, and what I learnt through my own journey, to some practical use. I got involved in an organisation called Drugarm for seven years. I did the training and went out on their Street Van, giving out food, drink and clothing. I befriended those who lived on the streets, at-risk youth and sex workers. I had been a person who was afraid of the dark, but God helped remove that fear and replaced it with strength, love and peace. I became a person who could sit under a very dark bridge in Henderson, late at night, at the foot of an elderly man living there.
Dealing with these people, my question was always, "What has brought them to this place?"

My passion is to bring hope to those without hope, to see the twinkle come back into their eyes. That is why I am here. It does not always matter how we came to be, what matters is that we were meant to be. In everyone, God has ordained a purpose. We are all unique and have a choice how we lead our lives.

My passion is to bring hope to those without hope

As well as doing volunteer work and raising our family, I trained and worked in the Mental Health sector for seven years. I loved my job supporting families. It was stressful and heart-breaking at times, but I also saw people gain a new lease of life with renewed hope when they got the right support around them. They went on to achieve goals and live a much more normal life. I learned so much during this time and have gained some valuable tools for helping people.

I have walked a long road of grace, forgiveness and healing. But how do others find some closure and healing? Where do they turn for help? Abortion is often a taboo subject, no one wants to talk about it or acknowledge the aftermath of abortion. So, to avoid judgement, too many struggle on their own. It becomes a deep dark secret which affects who they are. I really wanted to help others receive the healing I had experienced.

> I really wanted to help others receive the healing I had experienced

A little button says another precious button lived

I often thought of what could I do to make a difference in people's lives. I watched a documentary about the Paperclips project in America, where a class decided to collect paperclips to commemorate the loss of Jewish lives in the Holocaust. I was deeply moved. They received over 20 million paper clips, along with thousands of letters, and they created an incredible memorial. I then thought, I could do something similar! I chose the symbol of a button to represent a life taken. People who have had an abortion can no longer hold their baby and tell that lost child what they want to say, but they can hold a button. A button allows people to share their stories and to also create a memorial for their babies lost to abortion.

Helen Keller once said *"I am one, only one; I cannot do everything but I can do something".*

This was something Pete and I could do. So the Buttons Project was born in April 2008 out of our experience, to help others heal after their abortions and to bring their untold stories to light. My dream was—and remains—to collect thousands and thousands of buttons to create an amazing memorial. It will be a place to visit without judgement, a place to remember, to imagine, to grieve, and to then move on from with some peace and healing.

We often hear the abortion statistics, and we can become blasé when they talk of thousands and thousands of

Having something visual says so much more than a statistic

terminations. But you cannot be blasé when you see a single button and know that it represents a precious lost life, and with each button is a powerful story. Having something visual says so much more than a statistic. People send in their stories and comments with their special button. It is not only women who send them but often fathers, grandparents, siblings and friends—their grief is so often forgotten. This is the one thing they can do.

Why a button?

- It is easy to find and easy to send.
- It can be unique—representing a personal loss.
- It can symbolise closure, or security.
- Buttons are long-lasting, though fabric may fade or tear.
- Buttons join; buttons bring together. We are not alone.

So: you are wondering how many buttons do I have? Does it really matter—because even just one life is invaluable, and every story is unique and significant in itself—but so far I have been entrusted with over 20,000 buttons, and the number continues to grow.

> Even just one life is invaluable, and every story is unique

Some buttons have arrived anonymously. Some come carefully wrapped in tissue. Some are plain, some are handmade. Many come with stories and comments. Here are some typical ones:

"A small button for a small child—SIMON. Unwanted, unloved, unmourned and discarded in a back street abortion 58 years ago. Forgive me, little one. Your mother."

"I have not shared this life-changing, life destroying event with anyone who cares, and that is the biggest hurt. I don't think anyone else would care, for me or for the wee boy that I could not be a mother for. I am writing my story now. I wanted to thank you and Peter for your heartfelt story."

Others talked about how they spent quite a lot of time looking for just the right button, and others are yet to send in their button, awaiting a significant date.

Personally, I chose a button and named our baby 'Hope'. The button is for my baby, Hope, and for me. The button and her name represent hope for the future, peace now, and freedom from the past. It is for closure, and to commemorate something that was part of us.

It is for closure, and to commemorate something that was part of us

A voice

Word continues to spread about how the Buttons Project is collecting buttons to commemorate the babies whom we never met and creating a memorial for them. The Buttons Project: "What happened mattered, a way to remember, to grieve and to love." I feel deeply honoured by people sharing their stories with me and sending in their buttons.

> What happened mattered, a way to remember, to grieve and to love

I have held onto this proverb since starting to work in this area of abortion healing: *Speak up for those who cannot speak for themselves, for the rights of all who are destitute. Proverbs 31:8*

I want to be the voice. This is something I can do, to be a bridge towards healing and acknowledging what happened. The Buttons Project has been significant not just to myself, but to people of all ages who were not fully informed of the aftermath of abortion and the possible mental and physical dangers.

As I have gained my voice through this project, my story enables others to start their journey of healing and acknowledgment of what

> My story enables others to start their journey of healing

happened. It has been a great encouragement to me to
see word of the project spreading across the country and
beyond, reaching people of all walks of life.

Abortion often leads to a
deep private grief that is not
generally talked about. People
need to know they are not
alone as they start their journey
of healing and remembrance.
It takes great courage to share
such personal things. Because
these things are so private, all
the stories received into the
Buttons Project are treated with
great respect. I would never
jeopardize confidentiality—any stories I do share are
always anonymous or with explicit prior permission.
The stories and buttons inspire me to keep going, to be
a voice, to be able to reach more people, to bring hope
and healing.

> People need
> to know they
> are not alone
> as they start
> their journey
> of healing and
> remembrance

As well as the genuine pleasure I get in seeing people
healing emotionally, my involvement in the Buttons
Project ignites anger in me that women are still not
being fully informed. In the early weeks of pregnancy
it can be a very scary and daunting time. Abortion can
seem the quick fix but, as I know personally, and as
thousands of others have discovered, it is not. Women
need to know what support is available for them if
they choose life for their baby. It is not only support

throughout their pregnancy but, more importantly, after their baby is born.

My own experience, and that of many I have had contact with, is that the relief from the quick-fix of an abortion to solve an inconvenient or embarrassing problem is soon replaced by deep regret. The decision, often made in the heat of the moment and under pressure from others, usually fails to take into account the thing that haunts so many of us for years: this decision has ended the life of our own flesh and blood.

We are reaching many with our message but I believe we are just touching the tip of an iceberg. I am not a counsellor but I am someone with lived experience, a passion to help others and experience as a trained Mental Health Worker, and so I know the consequences can be serious. Abortion can lead to mental health problems. Often after an abortion there can be feelings of an emptiness, loss, depression, anxiety and low self-worth. Some even consider suicide. If serious mental health issues do arise after an abortion, I have found that abortion is rarely considered by psychologists or counsellors as a significant contributing factor. Her problems are more likely to be attributed to "a pre-existing mental condition."

After an abortion there can be feelings of an emptiness, loss, depression, anxiety and low self-worth

For many, abortion is a life-changing event. Abortion can harm women and yet there are individuals and groups who refuse to acknowledge this, or minimise it, seeming to place the right to obtain an abortion at a higher priority than the long-term health and welfare of women. There is much I could discuss with those people, and much we would probably disagree on, but I do want to say this: *"Whatever your beliefs are, we need to walk gently in people's lives as we do not know the journey someone has travelled, or the choices the woman had to choose from, that brought her to having an abortion."*

The project has opened the door to share with different community groups, youth, schools and church groups. I endeavour to speak whenever and wherever opportunity arises. I have been a spokesperson for Family First NZ, speaking up for both women's and babies' health and wellbeing and the impact of abortion. The important thing is to love them both, ensuring women are fully informed of the risks of abortion and know of the supports available to them throughout the pregnancy and after.

In 2014 I was deeply humbled to receive at Parliament the *Unsung Hero* award, presented by the NZ Christian

Network. The following year I got to speak to a Select Committee at Parliament. It was in relation to 'Hillary's Law—Parental Notification'. Young girls can get an abortion through their school without their parents being informed. It is the parents, however, who are left to pick up the pieces, often without knowing the reason behind the changes in their daughter's health, behaviour and emotions. I shared about the mental health of those affected by abortion. I said that our health system has let these young women down by failing to give them full information about the possible effects of abortion. They also short-change girls on information about other choices and support that is available.

> It is the parents who are left to pick up the pieces, often without knowing the reason behind the changes in their daughter's health, behaviour and emotions

The Buttons Project networks with a variety of organisations to help with post abortion recovery. For example, the Buttons Project started giving more support to facilitating the Living in Colour Post Abortion recovery programme. It has been amazing seeing women blossom and be restored through the programme.

When the Buttons Project had been going for a number of months, I got a phone call, out of the blue, from a guy called Richard. He and Roseanne ran a trust called Juxtaposition with the purpose of composing songs for organisations making a positive difference in their communities. Richard had been given one of my pamphlets, was moved by what we are doing and offered to write a song for Buttons. He even had some funding to do it! I was stunned and thought, "Wow! This is amazing!" So we all embarked on a journey of many discussions, back and forth, to write the song.

Richard also brought on board a woman from his church, Jackie, to help with the lyrics. She was a real blessing. Because she had been affected by having an abortion herself, this project was another stage in her own healing journey. Once we got the words and music together, we decided we then needed to make a good quality music video, which meant gathering a lot more funding. So we shared the vision of the project with many people and managed to get some more funds, as well as Pete and I contributing personally.

All those involved in the video had been affected in some way by abortion. They saw the song as a wonderful thing to help reach more people to help them find their healing and to let them know that they were not alone.

> Abortion is often like a deep wound, hidden, a secret shame, a scar on a person's soul

My husband and I believe the Buttons Project song to be a powerful tool to reach out to those who are affected by an abortion and who are having difficulty coming to terms with the loss of a baby. Abortion is often like a deep wound, hidden, a secret shame, a scar on a person's soul which lies deep within.

For many, seeing this video and hearing the song starts to uncover this secret part of them again. To only do that would be cruel but the video also holds out the real hope that they can heal and feel whole again. It gives the opportunity to acknowledge the baby and help start the journey of healing, to bring closure and hope. It introduces them to The Buttons Project, which commemorates the babies we never met—the unforgotten babies. It enables those who have been affected by abortion to "Do something, when there is nothing you can do."

The song reaches out to the people who may not have been able to be reached by other means, and it is being played on other websites around the world. For people in Christchurch, the video has an extra poignancy: many of the scenes were shot in iconic locations that were destroyed in the terrible 2010 earthquake that happened only a few months after filming.

Peter's perspective

Hi, we are adding my experience into the story from here, because as the saying goes, "It takes two to tango". We are both part of the unfolding story going forward and this is a chance to give a male perspective.

The proposal

Once Marina shared with me that she may be pregnant, a flood of thoughts occurred. We had been dating about a year and things were progressing well, life was good. Now there was a baby in the picture—wow. Excitement, trepidation, uncertainty—what to do?

> That's one thing I did right, proposing

I thought it over and decided I wanted to propose BEFORE confirming the pregnancy. Because I didn't want the baby to be the reason we married hanging over the rest of our lives. Yes, we loved each other, but were we ready for this next big step? Sort of. Such a big decision, and I only wanted to marry once, so this was important. That's one thing I did right, proposing.

I don't think I had a firm idea about abortion. I was pro-family and wanted to have a family, but always thought of that happening in a nice logical order somewhere out in the future: marriage—house—family.

I didn't know anyone who had an abortion, but found out later that it had happened in my family's past, and also more recently—an unfortunate repeating cycle.

The idea that having a baby early in our marriage would mean we would always struggle concerned me. I also had the idea that if you decided early, the foetus was still just a small blob, so any decision needed to be made urgently.

It was a lot to take in and, for both of us, our emotions were in a whirl. I got given advice: if we acted quickly and quietly it would be just a small blip on the road to a happy future. To my shame, we chose not to seek wider counsel. If I had, I might have heard other, better points of view.

So we decided to see the family doctor and find out what our options were. Doctors are the experts, after all. The doctor didn't mention any other options to help us make an

The doctor didn't mention any other options to help us make an informed decision

informed decision. Instead the doctor arranged a further appointment at the Epsom Day Clinic for a consultation. We would know more then and could decide with the facts at hand.

Epsom Day Clinic experience

It felt a bit surreal, but also like what you go through for a specialist treatment—you go to see the "experts". Their advice seemed to be that the abortion option was easy and normal, but it was time to act now.

The timeline from first knowing of the pregnancy, to visiting the doctor and then three days in a row at the Epsom Clinic, all happened so quickly but we were advised it was all for the best.

> Their advice seemed to be that the abortion option was easy and normal, but it was time to act now

The advice was, don't jump into parenting right now. Settle into marriage, then choose to have a family when we were both ready. It seemed sound advice, so we did it—to my shame. I hadn't comprehended Marina's family's past and how that weighed on her mind. We were now being enfolded in this close-knitted secret, but we thought it was the best thing to do: do it, then leave this unfortunate incident behind us and get back on our road to future happiness. I was completely naive to what was about to unfold.

I was completely naive to what was about to unfold

The engagement

Surely it must have been a happy exciting time — preparing for the big celebration ahead of our engagement? For us, it was a real low point in our journey. Swirling emotions, secrets, lies and half truths.

We had a short engagement, with pressures and expectations from all sides. As well, there was a growing realisation of what we had done. It dramatically struck home when a friend got pregnant at the same time but she decided to continue with the pregnancy.

Marina changed. I couldn't figure out the profound emotional turmoil that was happening in her life. Happy, then moody, uncertain for the first time about us as a couple, hating the gnawing effects of this secret that was consuming us. "Let's just get through this — get married and all will be well."

Marina changed. I couldn't figure out the profound emotional turmoil that was happening in her life

Little did I know that thirty years on, this (little) thing would remain as the biggest regret in my life.

The early years

Were we happily married? Yes—at times, for moments, but not always.

The abortion created a rift between us, a background to many of our arguments. I wanted to bury it as a mistake in our past and to move on; I did not understand the rollercoaster of emotions that stayed with Marina, or how deep the hurt was in her life.

In the early years I chose to not allow it to be something I would dwell on. The past is the past, push on to build a brighter future I thought, but the clouds never left us for long.

> The past is the past, push on to build a brighter future I thought, but the clouds never left us for long

The change in me

For me, it was while I was doing a short term mission in Fiji, volunteering with some building work, that a change in me started to take place. A journey of healing began.

I was listening to a guy being interviewed by James Dobson on the radio. He was sharing his abortion experience—asking forgiveness from God, repenting, acknowledging his part in the process and admitting to his mistakes. He also asked forgiveness from his girlfriend from those days.

This was a 'God moment' for me. I realised I needed healing and that I needed to do the same: To acknowledge my failings, admitting my mistakes and seeking Marina's (and Hope's) forgiveness, for not being their support and their protector in that situation. I, for the first time, was truly sorry and hated my behaviour and complicit choices.

This brought about the start of my healing journey, bringing it all out from the shadows and into the light of God's love. There was years of hurt to heal and a realisation that a life lost cannot be replaced by another.

Hope, I am forever sorry for treating you this way.

I love the words of this song of hope—Beauty for Ashes, by Crystal Lewis. It perfectly describes the journey I went through.

The chorus goes...
He gives,
Beauty for ashes—
There was no way I could undo what was done—the abortion had happened and only ashes were left.

Strength for fear—
I hated my weakness and decisions. I had hidden my secret shame of those choices for years.

Gladness for mourning—
I had to truly grieve a life lost. My decisions stopped a life before it got started.

Peace for despair—
It took a while, a long time in many ways, to come to the place of peace for despair. A journey of healing, both together with Marina and individually.

The song goes on to say...
When what you've done
keeps you from moving on—
Our marriage had been heading for the rocks until we worked through the unresolved grief and pain together. We didn't want to be part of the 75% whose relationships fail after an abortion.

> We didn't want to be part of the 75% whose relationships fail after an abortion

When fear wants to make itself a home in your heart—
Our secret had to be a secret no more. It started by being open to our family and close friends. Now that fear has left that home it had in our hearts.

Know that forgiveness brings wholeness and healing— Finally we were free to repair and rebuild our marriage. Since then our marriage has been renewed and set free.

God knows your need— Burying the abortion never worked. Just believe what He said and hand it all over to Him.

The Buttons Project is the beauty from the ashes in our life.

The Buttons Project is the beauty from the ashes in our life

The Buttons Project was born

As Marina said, we watched the Paperclip project movie and this formed Marina's idea about buttons for those lost to abortion. I agreed with Marina that it was a good idea, but I was still working through my personal shame for my actions. I wasn't ready to 'go public', so to speak. But Marina was undeterred and beavered away. Here was something she was passionate about, a chance to do something, so our mistakes were not repeated by others.

Over time I have been changed, by seeing the good, the healing

---

I have been changed, by seeing the restoration unfolding as the Buttons Project touched and changed lives

---

and the restoration unfolding as the Buttons Project touched and changed lives.

The abortion was an event, something I am most ashamed of, the thing I am least proud of in my life's journey, and yet, amazingly, the healing from that event has become something which brings peace, not just in our own lives, but to countless others as well.

To bring hope, where there is often no hope.

"I am so proud of you Marina. Well done, Honey. Let's keep shaking that tree of despair that holds so many people captive. Blessings and love always, Peter."

ReSources

Contact details and help in New Zealand

Whenever you see a button, remember the Buttons Project—What happened mattered, a way to remember, to grieve and to love. Helping towards healing from abortion.

You can watch the music video "Little Button," along with other video stories and support services on our website. There are both men's and women's post-abortion healing programmes available.
www.buttonsproject.org

Is abortion part of your story? If you would like to get in touch with me, you are most welcome to contact me via the website or email marina@buttonsproject.org

Do you have a special button and message to send? Please go to our Virtual Buttons Memorial
www.buttonsproject.org/buttonsmemorial

For updates on the Buttons Project, stories received, and events, please join us on:
www.facebook.com/buttonsproject
www.instagram.com/buttonsproject

Living in Colour is one of the programmes we facilitate. A healing and recovery programme for women who have experienced abortion.
https://livingincolour.nz

Living in Colour is an eight-week course that has been used successfully in many countries worldwide. It gently helps you process what was happening for you at that time, who was involved and the emotional impact of the decision. The final chapter celebrates the process of emerging from the 'grey zone' of unresolved loss into a life of greater colour and freedom. Some feedback:

"I highly recommend the Living in Colour program. It was transformative, and I feel that I have emerged from merely existing to experiencing joy, hope, and forgiveness." Living in Colour participant.

If you would like to find out more, visit the website or contact Marina at marina@buttonsproject.org All inquiries are dealt with in the strictest confidence.

Rachel's Vineyard Retreats
Healing the wounds of abortion
—one weekend at a time.
www.rachelsvineyard.org.nz

These weekend Retreats are an experience of emotional and spiritual healing for men and women whose lives have been touched by abortion. The experience of abortion can be very isolating. Among the comments made by Rachel's Vineyard Retreat participants are ones like this:

"The Retreat was like reaching safe ground. Something has shifted. I didn't know that I would feel so settled... I feel whole."

Contact: Wendy Hill—Retreat Facilitator info@ rachelsvineyard.org.nz
or Suzanne O'Rourke—Rachel's Vineyard Retreat Site Leader, suzanneor@gmail.com

Hapai Taumaha Hapūtanga, Crisis Pregnancy Support Nelson/Tasman
Contact free call 0800 004 277
Wairarapa Contact free call 0800 006 277
www.crisispregnancysupport.org.nz

Pregnancy Choice NZ
Ph 0800 773 424 or text 027 222 8871
www.pregnancychoice.org.nz

My Buddy My Choice
https://myvoice.nz
A platform for men to share their stories, get resources, and embark on the healing journey.

Where to get help internationally

www.buttonsproject.org.au

www.buttonsproject.org.uk

www.rachelsvineyard.org

www.rachelsvineyard.org.au

Support after Abortion
https://supportafterabortion.com

We offer compassionate support for those impacted by abortion, and practical training and resources for those helping them heal.

Pregnancy Problem House
https://www.pregnancyproblemhouse.org.au
Support for individuals experiencing unintended or unsupported pregnancies, as well as healing after an abortion.

Victims of abortion (Australia)
https://www.victimsofabortion.com.au

The Stacy Zallie Foundation
www.stacyzallie.org
Assisting women who have made the difficult choice of ending their pregnancy in finding a caring, non-judgmental resource to help restore their happiness and reconnect with their loved ones and their future.

Project Rachel
Post Abortion Healing Ministry
https://hopeafterabortion.com

Men and Abortion
www.menandabortion.net

Crossroads Pregnancy Centre (America)
https://crossroadswomenscenter.com

Abortion Recovery Care and Help (United Kingdom)
https://www.archtrust.org.uk

Stand up girl
www.standupgirl.com

For young women who find themselves with an unplanned pregnancy. Also, for women affected by having an abortion and supports available to help towards healing.

Research on Abortion

*"Abortion is such a life-changing event for many.
I believe we are just touching the tip of an iceberg.
Abortion can harm women—yet there are groups who
refuse to acknowledge this, seeing the right to abortion
more paramount than the long-term health and welfare
of the women." Marina—Buttons Project*

**Abortion and the Physical & Mental Health
of Women:** A review of the evidence for health
professionals. *Dr Gregory Pike: Adelaide Centre for
Bioethics and Culture.*

https://familyfirst.org.nz/wp-content/
uploads/2021/03/Abortion-and-the-Physical-Mental-
Health-of-Women-2021.pdf

Abortion is associated with a wide range of adverse
physical and psychological outcomes.

Professor David Fergusson and his team of
researchers, from the University of Otago's
Christchurch Health and Development, did a study
which aimed to examine the linkages between having
an abortion and mental health outcomes over the
interval from age 15-25 years.

www.ncbi.nlm.nih.gov/pubmed/16405636

Those having an abortion had elevated rates of subsequent mental health problems including depression, anxiety, suicidal behaviours and substance use disorders. The findings suggest that abortion in young women may be associated with increased risks of mental health problems. Professor Ferguson did a follow-up study in the women until the age of 30, that major mental health problems in those who had abortions were about 30 percent higher than in women not having abortions.

Study: Abortion's Long-Term Negative Impact on Men. *By Greg Mayo April 2023*

Greg Mayo is an author and speaker. He wrote the book 'Almost Daddy" https://supportafterabortion. com/wp-content/uploads/2022/07/Support-After-Abortion-Mens-Research-White-Paper-VF1.pdf

Support After Abortion research shows that for seven out of ten men, abortion is a painful experience that can include emotional distress and lasting feelings of loss and grief.

Priscilla Coleman, in the British Journal of Psychiatry (2011), published research on abortion and mental health. http://bjp.rcpsych.org/content/199/3/180

The results revealed a moderate to highly increased risk of mental health problems after abortion.

A study in China, The Impact of Prior Abortion on Anxiety and Depression Symptoms During Subsequent Pregnancy: Data from a Population-Based Cohort Study in China, by Huang, Hao, Su, Kun Huang, Xing, Cheng,Xiao, Xu, Zhu, Tao, published in Bulletin of Clinical Psychopharmacology 2012:22(1)51-58. www.psikofarmakoloji.org/pdf/22_1_8.pdf

Conclusions: These results suggest women who have experienced a previous induced abortion have omnipresent anxiety and depression symptoms during a subsequent pregnancy, especially during the first trimester.

Hush: The documentary

A liberating conversation about abortion and women's health, which can be viewed online. Well worth the watch. www.hushfilm.com